The People's Hist

Hetton-le-Hole
and District

by

Geoffrey Berriman

A Hetton Lyons Colliery Vertical Boilered Steam Locomotive in 1905. It was constructed using parts of a marine engine.

Previous page: Hetton miners marching along Caroline Street to their Annual Service on 23rd May 1957.

Copyright © Geoffrey Berriman 2002

First published in 2002 by

The People's History Ltd
Suite 1
Byron House
Seaham Grange Business Park
Seaham
Co. Durham
SR7 0PY

ISBN 1 902527 66 6

Contents

C. Carter, Driver, and his Fireman, standing
next to their engine at Hetton Lyons Colliery,
circa 1940.

*I wish to dedicate this book to my aunt Ethel Thompson (née Berriman) who
has given me great encouragement in the compilation of it and other books.*

Introduction

It has been a pleasure to compile this book on Hetton-le-Hole and adjacent villages.

In Pigot and Company's *Pocket Atlas, Topography and Gazetteer of England* published in 1821 Hetton-le-Hole is described as:

'...village and township in the Parish of Houghton-le-Spring, about two miles S (south) from that town and six NE (north east) from Durham situated in an agreeable vale. Not twenty years ago the population of Hetton did not exceed five hundred persons; at that period a colliery was commenced by the late Hon Captain Cochrane RN and partners, which of late years has so much increased in value, and employed so many work people, that it is estimated there are now eight thousand individuals chiefly dependent upon it ...'

The district witnessed considerable further development of coal mining, and also the very early development of the railways. The last coal mine closed in 1985, and Hetton Colliery Railway Line in 1959, but fortunately good photographic records exist, and I hope that the photographs I have included will bring back memories for some people as well as giving others a picture of aspects of life which were so important in previous generations.

What has struck me about the Hetton of today is the strong evidence of a very positive spirit in the community. There are thriving voluntary organizations and well patronised independent local businesses. I have also tried to include some record of the area as it is now as well as of long ago.

Form 2 of Hetton Council School (later Hetton Lyons), *circa* 1912. Note the hair ribbons.

Hetton School Band entertaining at the Senior Citizens' Party held at the school, December 2001.

Acknowledgements

In compiling this book I have been fortunate in receiving generous help from many people, both in the provision of photographs and information. I would therefore like to thank the following: Beamish Museum; the Revd Michael Beck, Vicar of Hetton and Eppleton; the Managing Director and Staff of Blendex Foods Ltd; Mrs J. Buckingham, Hetton Silver Band; Mrs Lena Cooper; Mr George Defty; Durham County Record Office; Eppleton Primary School; the Revd D. Guest; Mr Morgan Hardy; Eleanor Harvey; Mr Mel Heslop; Hetton Community Centre; Mr Shaun Newton, Hetton Independent Methodist Church; Hetton Lyons School; Hetton Methodist Church; Hetton School; Hetton Town Council; Mrs Y. Hickman; Pamela Linge; Dr Derek Lodge; Mr Peter Lodge FRCS; Miss Y. Moor; Mr George Nairn; Mrs C. Ritchie, E. & N. Ritchie; Mr Sparrow; Mr W. Stabler; Mrs M. Tate, Moorsley Community Association; and Mr Dennis Tomys of Hetton Picture Framing.

I should also like to thank Mr Andrew Clark of The People's History for his usual helpfulness while I have been compiling the book.

THE TOWN OF
HETTON-LE-HOLE

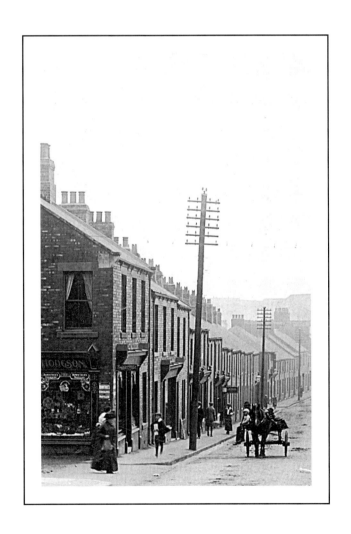

Front Street, Hetton, *circa* 1900. The second building from the right is still the Brewer's Inn today. To the left of it is a dressmaker's shop, now Ladbrokes. While taking photographs for this book I was stopped by a family in a car who asked me if I knew the origins of the name of Hetton-le-Hole. I had to confess I did not, but I then carried out some research which suggests that Hetton-le-Hill meant the hill where Hips grew and that Hetton-le-Hole was at the foot of the hill or in the valley.

A similar view of Front Street in 2002. The town house on the far right in the earlier picture has been altered considerably and now forms Gill's Golden Fry and Pizzamatic. The public house and the building immediately to the left of it can be clearly seen in the older photograph.

Front Street, Hetton, *circa* 1905. This presents a rural village scene. On the far left is the school originally known as The National and Barrington School (now part of Gateway Supermarket). The Post Office can be seen left centre, and the Infants School centre right (now the Library). The building second from the right was occupied by the London & Newcastle Tea Company.

A similar view of Front Street from a similar angle in 2002.

The Post Office in the late 1930s. The building to the left with the clock was once used as offices by Hetton Urban District Council. Below the clock is a plaque with an inscription which reads: 'Township of Hetton-le-Hole, Great War 1914-18. This clock is erected to the memory of the fallen Sailors and Soldiers in the above War, August 1922.'

The Post Office, Front Street in 2002.

Bleach Green Bank, Hetton, *circa* 1903. The building on the right was originally the Conservative Club, and the foundation stone reads: 'This foundation stone was laid by A.N. Lindsay Wood Saturday May 30th 1896.' It has now been the home of Hetton Social Club for many years. St Nicholas' Church can be seen in the middle, and the building on the left is the present day premises of E. & N. Ritchie, Motor Engineers.

The view from a similar angle today. In this photograph St Nicholas' Church has been entirely obscured by trees. Buildings erected since the previous photograph include the Masonic Hall and the houses between the club and the trees on the right.

Station Road, Hetton, *circa* 1915. The shop on the left was A.W. Hodgson, Greengrocer and Confectioner. Note the rails and overhead lines for trams on the right. Trams ran in Hetton from 1905 to 1924.

Station Road, Hetton in 2002. Hodgson's shop is now S. & A. King, Quality Grocer and Delicatessen.

A view of Market Street, Hetton Downs, *circa* 1903. Still containing many shops today it was a very busy shopping area in the late 19th century and first half of the 20th century.

View of Market Street in 2002.

Another view of Market Street, *circa* 1919.

Francis Street which was demolished in the 1970s lay in between Regent Street and Edward Street. Some of the Francis Street cottages can be seen at Beamish, the North of England Open Air Museum, where they were rebuilt as good examples of typical miners' cottages of the late 19th and early 20th centuries

Four Lane Ends, Hetton, *circa* 1903.

Four Lane Ends in 2002. Many of the cottages shown in the top photograph have been demolished, but the New Inn is still a popular public house.

Front Street, Hetton, *circa* 1954.

Front Street in 2002. Little appears to have changed since the time of the top photograph.

A postcard view of Front Street, Hetton, *circa* 1940. Far left is the Golden Lion Hotel. The card written in 1943 during wartime reads: 'Having a nice time here and weather fairly good. The fish shops round here are terribly busy. Betty waited over an hour for some last night …'

Front Street in 2002. The Golden Lion Hotel and two adjacent shops have been demolished. Other buildings in the top picture still stand but some of the shops have been substantially altered.

The Caroline public house and Caroline Street, Hetton, *circa* 1972.

Caroline Street in 2002. The Caroline remains a popular public house. Many of the houses shown on the left in the top photograph have been demolished and replaced with new houses.

Front Street, Hetton, *circa* 1948.

A view of Low Downs Square, Hetton in the early 1960s. These houses were later demolished.

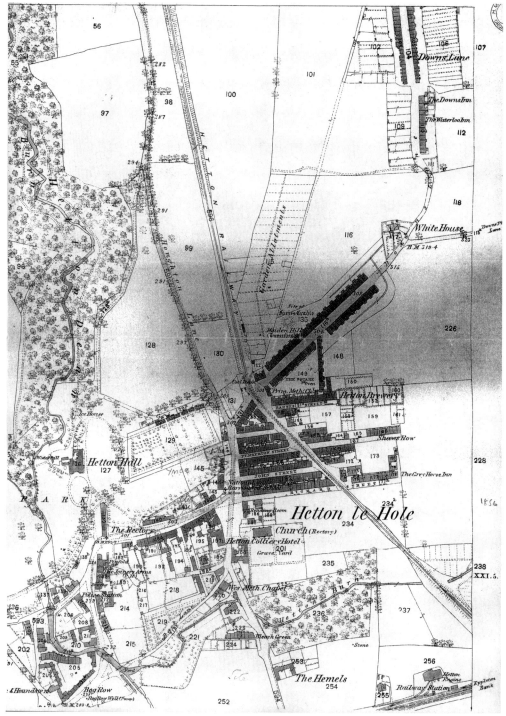

Reproduced from the Ordnance Survey Map 1856. A magnifying glass might help readers to identify some of the houses and streets still standing now. Hetton Colliery Railway Line can be clearly seen.

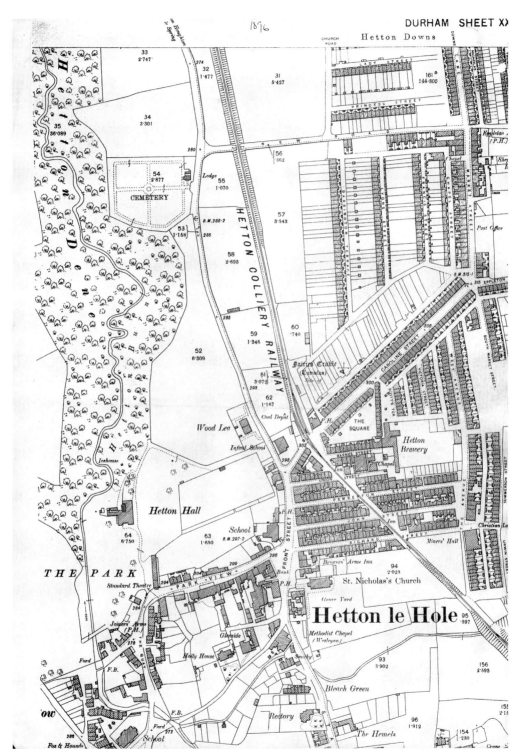

Reproduced from the Ordnance Survey Map 1896. Note that with the expansion of the mines a large amount of new housing had been built in the forty years since the date of the previous map.

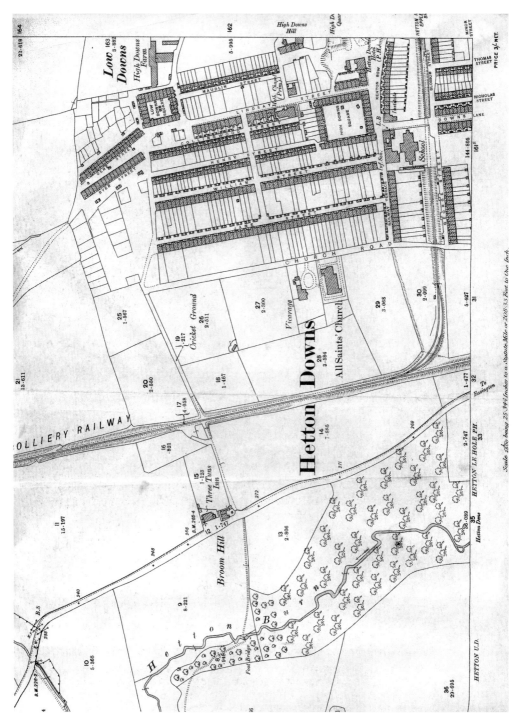

Reproduced from the Ordnance Survey Map 1896, Hetton Downs or Eppleton. Note the route of the Hetton Colliery Railway. Many of the houses shown at the top of the map have been demolished but some of the replacement housing erected in the 1950s and '60s has retained the old street names, such as Blossom Street, High Downs Square and George Street.

Bog Row, Hetton, 2002. On the left below the railings can be seen the stone retaining wall which forms part of a raised area known as The Quay.

Edward Street on the left and Fairy Street on the right. The grass in the middle covers what was once the well known landmark of the 'Fairies' Cradle'. A hundred years or so before the houses were built, Surtees remarked in his History that: 'In a field on the right hand side of the road from Eppleton to Hetton, and only one field from Houghton-lane, is a remarkable tumulus, consisting entirely of field-stones gathered together. At the top there is a small oblong hollow, called the Fairies' Cradle: on this little green mound, which has always been sacred from the plough, Village – superstition believes the Fairies to have led their moonlight circles, and whistled their roundelays to the wind.'

The Council Offices in 2002. These house the City of Sunderland Hetton Area Office and the Town Council Offices. Prior to 1974 the building served as offices for Hetton Urban District Council, and prior to that use was a Doctor's house.

The Cottage, a well and sympathetically restored set of buildings in Park View.

Old Brewery Inn, *circa* 1905. The inn stood near the Union Street Methodist Church which can be seen in the background.

The former King's Head public house in Richard Street has been used in recent years as a meeting place and community centre for elderly people. The Hetton Colliery Line ran very close by, and in recent years the building has been known as Stephenson House after George Stephenson the great railway engineer. If you look at the glass pane above the front door you will see the effigy of a King in the style of a King in a pack of cards, a reminder of the building's past.

On the left of the picture is the premises of Jack Guy, Blacksmith and Horse
Shoer on North Road, Hetton. Now closed, the sign remains. Many Hetton
people will remember this busy Smithy.

A scene in Front Street, Hetton, 2001.

HETTON COAL MINING DAYS

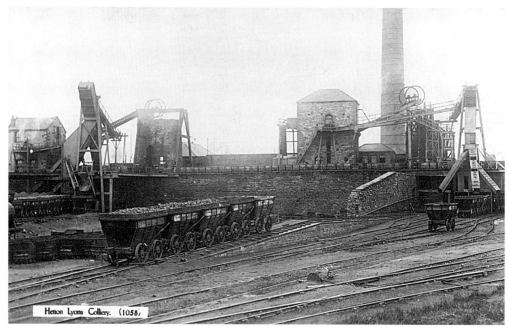

Hetton Lyons Colliery, *circa* 1903. The pit was first sunk in 1818 but work was stopped by quicksand. A successful working was carried out in 1821-22. The pit closed in 1950.

Another view of Hetton Lyons Colliery of the same period.

A further view of Hetton Lyons Colliery.

Miners of Hetton Lyons Colliery, *circa* 1900.

Above: Miners at Hetton Lyons Colliery, *circa* 1920.

Left: Hetton Lyons Colliery Electricians in 1948. Most private collieries were nationalised in 1948 to form the National Coal Board.

Eppleton Pit known as the New Pit, *circa* 1903. The pit was sunk in the 1820s and closed in 1985.

Eppleton Colliery in the early 1980s.

Sir Lindsay Wood who was born in 1834 was the Managing Director of the Hetton Coal Company Limited from 1865 to 1911. He was the son of Nicholas Wood, George Stephenson's business partner.

Ralph Cochrane who was a prominent citizen in Hetton in the late 19th and early 20th centuries. He was Company Secretary of the Hetton Coal Company, a Poor Law Guardian and a member of Hetton Urban District Council.

Mr Sam Watson, the highly respected Durham Miners' Leader, making presentations to retired miners, 20th July 1951.

Eppleton Miners' Lodge Officials with the Lodge Banner, *circa* 1979.

A view of Eppleton Colliery, *circa* 1900.

The second incline bankhead or Wet Cut on the Hetton Colliery Railway, *circa* 1900.

SECTION THREE

COMMERCE AND THE WORKPLACE

Above: The Post Office, Front Street, *circa* 1905.

Left: The Chop Suey House, Market Street, 2002, with proprietors Mrs Hailing Liang and Mr Dahein Tran.

Shop of J. Coxon & Co, General Merchants, Market Street, Hetton, *circa* 1905.

The Barber's Shop at 1 Front Street, Hetton, was established in 1892. This picture was taken in 2002.

Staff outside the premises of John Speed, Tobacconists, 7 Richard Street, *circa* 1952.

The corner of Front Street and Park View, Hetton, *circa* 1915.

The corner of Front Street and Park View 2002.

Right: Hetton
Picture Framing in
Front Street. The
proprietor, Mr
Dennis Tomys, was
formerly the Post
Master at Hetton.

Below: Stevenson's
Pets and Miami
Tanning, Front
Street, Hetton,
2002.

Above: S. & A. King, Quality Grocer and Delicatessen, Station Road, Hetton, 2002.

Left: J.A. & J.A. Slater, Newsagents, Confectioners and Tobacconist, Station Road, 2002.

Right: Norman Lodge (left) and Mr E. Wild (right) outside Mr Wild's Dental Practice at Station Road, *circa* 1910. Norman Lodge was then a schoolboy and used to help Mr Wild. After service in the First World War he qualified as a Dentist himself, later taking over Mr Wild's Practice. Many Hetton citizens will remember Mr Lodge.

Below: The Hetton Dental Practice of Mr Ellis and Mr Farnell at Station Road in 2002.

The Refuge Assurance Company's District Office at 55 Station Road, *circa* 1915.

The premises of G. Fenton & Son, Electrical Contractors, Station Road, in 2002.

Above: Hunter &
Co, Confectioners,
Tobacconists and
Hairdressers, 53
Market Street, *circa*
1935. The building
is now occupied by
Hetton Downs Post
Office.

Right: Hetton
Downs Post Office,
53 Market Street, in
2002.

JD's Cottage Sandwich Shop, Bog Row, Hetton, 2002 – selling hot and cold sandwiches, snacks, drinks, confectionery and ice cream. I was given very cheerful service when I bought a sandwich here.

My Abu Sufian Choudhury and Ms Joanne Wilson outside the Spicey Balti Indian Take Away, Market Street, 2002.

Staff of G.W. Sparrow, Building Contractor, Hetton, *circa* 1925.

Mr Joe Lormor (left) and Mr David Hall (second right) of Lormor & Hall Construction, Hetton-le-Hole, with two members of staff, 2002.

Mr Willis Hudson Piper outside the firm's Hetton shop in 2002. The firm was founded in 1890 by Mr Piper's great-grandfather and is a good example of a number of thriving, long established, independent businesses in the district. The strong sun on the day I took the photograph has blurred the shop sign. My apologies.

Gordon's Shop, Hetton, *circa* 1955. It stood on the site where the Gateway Supermarket is now.

SECTION FOUR

HIGH AND LOW MOORSELY AND GREAT AND LITTLE EPPLETON

A procession of the North Hetton Miners' Lodge, *circa* 1880. The Banner, depicting the Good Samaritan, contained the biblical quotation from St Matthew, Chapter 7, verse 12: 'Whatsoever ye would that men do unto you, do ye also unto them.'

Another view of North Hetton Colliery, *circa* 1880. Limestone would have been quarried from the rock formation right foreground for burning in the kilns left foreground. None of the buildings now exists but there is still evidence of the limestone quarrying.

A winter view
of North Hetton
Colliery, *circa*
1880.

A view of
North
Hetton
Colliery at
Low
Moorsley,
circa 1880.
This colliery
opened in
1825 and
closed in
1925.

Laying drains at North Hetton Colliery, *circa* 1880. The colliery was owned by the North Hetton Coal Company which also manufactured bricks, and fire clay products, of which the drains in the photograph were possibly examples.

Another view of North Hetton Colliery, Moorsley, *circa* 1880. The building mid background is believed to be one of the two Methodist Chapels which Low Moorsley had at this period.

A van being built for Low Moorsley Amicable Industrial Society at Houghton Carriage Works, *circa* 1905.

Moorsley Community Association provides a variety of activities for the village. Pictured outside is Mr W. Stabler, 2002.

The Old Limestone Quarry workings at Low Moorsley are still visible, July 2002.

The former Methodist Chapel, Low Moorsley, in 2001. The chapel was built in 1858 and now serves as a storage yard. Low Moorsley also had another Methodist Church but this has been demolished. It was possibly the building mentioned in the caption to the bottom photograph on page 50.

Above: Interior of St Oswald's Mission Church, High Moorsley, *circa* 1910. The church closed in 1970 and has since been demolished.

Right: The Revd George Gibson who was curate of the Rainton-cum-Moorsley Mission Church 1891-93. He later became Rector of Ebchester, Co Durham, and was a prolific author and journalist.

Left: The former Moorsley School is now a private house, but the shape of the school is still evident, and the original school walls and gateways can be seen at the front of the photograph.

Right: Valley View, Low Moorsley, in 2002. Some of the best views in the North East of England are to the north and north west.

Near the top of the hill at High Moorsley. Mackenzie & Ross in their 1834 book *Historical, Typographical, and Descriptive View of the County Palatine of Durham*, described Moorsley as: 'a small village on a high, bare brow, overlooking the vale of Houghton.' They said the name Moorsley was derived from 'Moreslaw' (the Moor-hill). This photograph taken in 2002 shows some of the few remaining buildings from the earlier village which included two public houses, one of which, The Lamb public house, is now the house on the left.

The Old Hall, Great Eppleton. Demolished in the early 20th century it is uncertain when it was first built but there was a Manor of Epplyngdene here in the 12th century.

The fine Hall at Little Eppleton in the late 1950s. This substantial country house is divided into several separate houses. Surtees in his History records that in the 17th century the house here was originally known as Eppleton Field House. Major architectural changes have taken place since then.

Mr and Mrs George Moor of Great Eppleton with their son John (on the pony) and their daughter Annie May, *circa* 1907. The Moor family started farming at Throughgate Farm, Great Eppleton, in the late 1870s, and they still have the farm today.

Throughgate Farm House at Great Eppleton.

Throughgate Farm at Great Eppleton in the early 1980s. The buildings had reached the end of their life and were subsequently demolished and replaced. There are a number of long established farms in the Hetton district which survived the industrialisation of the nineteenth and twentieth century, and have contributed to much of the attractive landscape which can be seen throughout the district.

Another scene at Throughate Farm, Great Eppleton, in the 1980s.

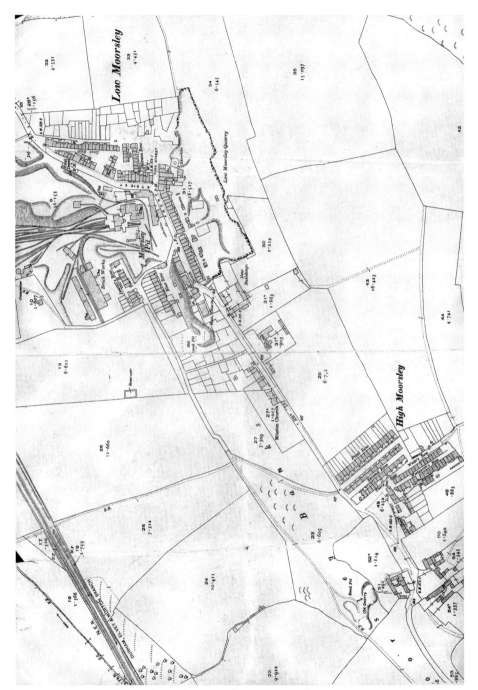

Ordnance Survey, Low and High Moorsley, 1896. There was considerable industry in Low Moorsley with the Pit (North Hetton Colliery), Brickworks and Quarry. Many Collieries in the area had adjacent Brickworks because of the large clay deposits. Very few of the buildings on the map exist today. Some of them are shown on the following pages. In High Moorsley there were five rows of houses and a front street, the only surviving building among these being the former public house, The Lamb, which is now a private house.

A MISCELLANY OF HETTON PEOPLE AND HETTON LIFE

From the right, Mr George Defty, his daughter Jane, and a confectionery firm representative outside 9 Richard Street, *circa* 1930.

Number 9 Richard Street is still lived in by Mr George Defty's descendants. His grandson (right) and his great-grandson, both also called George, outside 9 Richard Street in 2002.

The former Police Station in Station Road, Hetton. Today it forms part of Hetton House Residential Care Home.

Aged Miners' Homes along North Road, Hetton. These are typical of cottages built for retired miners in County Durham in the first three decades of the 20th century. The cottages in the photograph were part of a group which were officially named The William  Robinson J.P. Memorial Homes and were opened by Sir Lindsay Wood on 11th March 1916. A large number of foundation stones were usually laid by local dignitaries. Two of these can be seen at the base of the cottage on the far left. There is also a later dedication stone higher up on the left just under the street sign. Its inscription reads: 'Erected as a Memorial to Captain The Honourable Sydney James Drever Joicey and the Sailors, Soldiers and Airmen of the Hetton Urban District who fell in the Great War 1914-18.' The Joicey family like the Wood family were very well known coal mine owners.

A reunion of Hetton Special Constables, 1949.

Hetton St John Ambulance Garden Fête, June 1950.

Hetton County Workmen's Club Fur and Feather Show, November 1952.

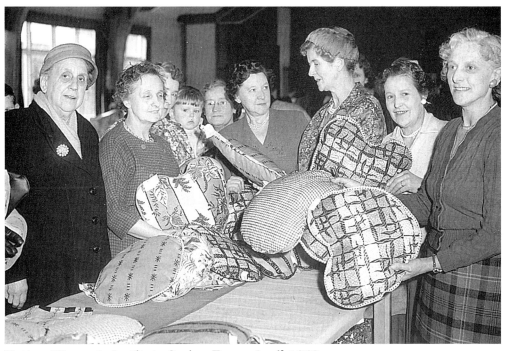

Hetton Women's Institute Spring Fayre, April 1969.

Freemasons in the Masonic Hall, Hetton-le-Hole, 30th December 1954.

The Road Safety Queen giving a demonstration at Hetton in 1952.

Hetton Comrades Social Club Opening in 1956. The building in Houghton Road is now The Croft Club.

Pensioners Leek and Vegetable Show, Hetton, 1952.

Ponies at the Hetton Agricultural Show in 1959. The show is no longer held, but its existence was demonstrative of the strong links an industrial town retained with the area's agriculture.

Horse Floats at Hetton Agricultural Show, August 1959.

Blendex Food Ingredients Ltd on Hetton Lyons Industrial Estate in 2002. Blendex prepares herb and spice mixes and distributes them to the food industry nationally and internationally. Additional new premises on the Estate are currently being built for the company. The Industrial Estate is on the site of Hetton Lyons Colliery.

Presentation of a cup to Hetton Lyons School athlete, Joy Hodgson, 1958.

Crossing the ford at Ford Lane, Hetton, 2002.

Hetton Park has long been a popular and pleasant walk. The Park formerly formed part of the grounds of Hetton Hall which was demolished in 1923. In Volume 1 of his History of the County Palatine of Durham published in 1816, Surtees notes that: 'The Mansion-house stands low, to the west of the Village, surrounded by soft wooded grounds, and almost on the edge of a sheet of water formed by the Hetton-Burn. The Dene, through which the stream afterwards falls, is thickly planted, and affords some close wood walks.' The Hall is portrayed on Eppleton Miners' Banner.

Above: The Imperial Cinema in Railway Street. Now demolished, it stood next to Hetton Workingmen's Club and Institute. In March 1930 it showed *The Tale of Lost Ships*, the first talking picture seen in Hetton.

Right: The Pavilion Works in Richard Street formerly housed the Pavilion Cinema which closed in the 1960s.

This building in Park View now used by G.W. Wright, Suppliers of Agricultural Feeds, was formerly the Standard Theatre.

Members of the Eppleton and Houghton-le-Spring Bowls Teams, June 1949.

Right: Eppleton Quarry, *circa* 1972. The quarry has long been a supplier of limestone for building purposes.

Below: The Old Smithy which stood near the burn on the opposite side of Front Street to the Masons' Hall. The buildings at the front of the photograph to the right of the tree have now been demolished.

Left: A Hetton resident with his dog behind Market Street, July 2002. When taking photographs, it has been my pleasure to meet many friendly Hetton people.

Below: Hetton & District Workingmen's Club, *circa* 1930. The Band Stand is no longer there. The First World War Memorial stands on the right. Among the names on the memorial is that of local war hero Company Sergeant Major Michael Bond who was decorated with the Military Medal and Bar and who also received the Russian Order of St George for conspicuous bravery in the field of battle. In the background is St Nicholas' Church.

WORKMEN'S CLUB, HETTON-LE-HOLE.

Hetton and District Workingmen's Club after the fire in 1957.

Hetton & District Workingmen's Club in 1958 after restoration work.

These old buildings in Office Place, Hetton, are now used as a street cleaning depot by Sunderland City Council. The roof would have been originally tiled with clay pantiles which were common in the area before the arrival of slates.

Hetton Club Ambulance Team 1914.

This photograph taken in July 2002 shows a new private housing development under construction at Eppleton just behind Houghton Road.

The same housing development nearing completion in September 2002.

A view of the large man made Lyons Lake in Hetton Lyons Country Park. This is fed from existing streams and forms part of Sunderland City Council's reclamation scheme for the area.

The new Community Centre, at the south west end of the football ground off Park View, nearing completion in September 2002.

Hetton Handicapped Persons' Social Club, 1960.

Hetton High Downs Christmas Fayre, December 1959.

Hetton Lyons Boys' Club in the 1960s. The building, near Lyons Cottages, still stands, though the club closed some years ago. Originally, the building was the first of the engine sheds for the Hetton Colliery Railway.

Queen Elizabeth, The Queen Mother, receiving a posy from Dorothy Heslop at the opening of the Hetton Lyons Boys Club in 1965. On the right is Mr Douglas Nicholson, Chairman of Vaux Breweries and Chairman of County Durham Boys' Clubs.

Queen Elizabeth, The Queen Mother, meeting Mr J. Heslop, Honorary Secretary, at the opening of the Hetton Lyons Boys' Club in 1965. In the middle is the Reverend Bell, Vicar of Lyons. The Queen Mother was felt to have a special connection with Hetton. She was born Elizabeth Bowes Lyon, daughter of the Earl of Strathmore. Land at Hetton came into the Lyon family early in the 18th century when it was sold by the Spearman family to the then Dowager Countess of Strathmore.

The singing star Dusty Springfield visits Hetton Lyons Boys' Club, *circa* 1965.

Members of an earlier Hetton Lyons Boys' Club in 1941. Mr J. Heslop, who later became Honorary Secretary of the new club, can be seen in Air Training Corps' uniform third from right standing.

Thomas and Eleanor Dolphin outside their home in Lyons Avenue, Hetton-le-Hole. Thomas Dolphin was Master Mason at the Lyons Colliery from approximately 1883 to 1913. In 1913 they and their four sons went to Australia, but following the outbreak of the First World War the family returned to Hetton in 1915. Thomas Dolphin took up employment as Master Mason at the Brickworks and worked there until he died at the age of 83 in 1927. Unaware of his death Eleanor died three hours after husband and a joint funeral was held for them.

The opening of Hetton Community Centre, 18th September 1972 by County Councillor G.W. Davidson (centre). On the left is Mr Charles Grey, a Hetton man, who was the MP for Durham and Chairman of the Centre. On the right is Mr Harry Bunker.

Mr Jack Daglish outside his pigeon loft near Eppleton Quarry in the mid 1970s. This traditional hobby is maintained by many enthusiasts in the district today.

The Chairman of Hetton Town Council, Councillor A.R. Wilkinson, in front of the Eppleton Lodge Banner prior to participating in the Durham Miners' Gala, July 2002. The Banner shows Hetton Hall and a locomotive built by the celebrated engineer George Stephenson for the Hetton Colliery Company in the 1820s.

Members of Hetton Town Council in 2002. The Chairman, Councillor A.R. Wilkinson (third left front row) and the Clerk, Mr John Price (far right back row).

CHURCHES AND CHAPELS

Left: A photograph of the Anglican Church in Hetton which was built in 1831. It was demolished in the late 19th century and replaced on the same site by the present Church of St Nicholas.

Below: St Nicholas' Church, Hetton, *circa* 1915. The sender of this postcard had written to the person to whom he was sending it: 'I walked 14 miles to get this card. I don't know whether you deserve it.'

HETTON CHURCH. 1064.

The interior of St Nicholas' Church, Hetton, *circa* 1910 .

On the left the Anglican church of St Nicholas in Front Street, Hetton. The church was designed by Stephen Piper and dates from 1901. Pevsner in the first edition of the County Durham volume in his celebrated  series on the Buildings of England gives the church this description: 'A good picturesque w (west) front with, on the ground floor, a Baptistery with three parallel gables, and above it a group of five lancets under a gable. Gabled buttresses; bellcote. The interior with tall, square, slightly chamfered piers and arches high up dying into them.' Unfortunately the church has now been closed for services due to the state of the building. Services are now held in the Church Hall. Fixed on St Nicholas House, one of the two houses adjacent to the Church, is a plaque which reads: 'Nicholas Wood 1795-1865 Colliery Viewer (Engineer) and Partner of George Stephenson, Wood lived here during the sinking of Hetton Lyons Pit. His grave is in the adjacent churchyard.' Wood and Stephenson were responsible for the production of the famous Puffing Billy engines. After living in this house he lived in Hetton Hall and was elected a fellow of the Royal Society.

The Union Street Methodist Church, Hetton, which dates from 1858. The larger dark stones used in the building are old stone sleepers from Hetton Colliery Railway which ran nearby. A coffee morning is held at the church every Saturday, and I was given a very friendly welcome at one by members of the congregation who showed me round.

The west elevation of Hetton Methodist Church. When I took this photograph a flock of seagulls had obligingly landed on the roof ridge to give a decorated effect.

Interior of Union Street Methodist Church taken from its fine gallery.

Hetton Methodist Church Choir in 1970. Every Good Friday the Church performs an Oratorio and these have featured many well known soloists.

Members of Hetton Boys Brigade, a Methodist Youth Organisation, in the grounds of Hetton Hall, *circa* 1913. They had built the wooden bridge seen in the photograph.

The Wesleyan Methodist Chapel, Front Street. No longer a chapel, it was first erected in 1824, and subsequently enlarged. To its left is the former Wesleyan School, now the Service Centre.

Engraving of the Revd W.R. de Winton (Methodist Minister) on his tombstone in Hetton Cemetery. The inscription reads: 'Tombstone erected by a sympathetic public in loving memory of the Reverend W.R. de Winton, Primitive Methodist Minister of the Hetton Circuit for over six years who lost his life during a gale February 27th 1903.'

Members of Hetton Independent Methodist Church, *circa* 1929. The Church was founded in the 1880s by 'Christ's Army', a group which had split from the Salvation Army. The actual church building was opened on 31st August 1889.

Some of the congregation at Hetton Independent Methodist Church after morning service on 14th April 2002. I received another friendly welcome here when I came to take this photograph.

A concert at Hetton Independent Methodist Church in July 2001.

Hetton Independent Methodist Church Members with Mrs Elizabeth Patterson on her 90th birthday in 1949.

Members of the congregation celebrating the 70th Anniversary of All Saints, Eppleton.

View of the Old Vicarage, Eppleton, with All Saints Church in the background.

All Saints Church, Eppleton. The foundation stone was laid in the presence of Lord Londonderry and members of the Bowes-Lyon family on 2nd November 1886 by Mrs Lindsay Wood, wife of the Managing Director of the Hetton Coal Company.

SCHOOLDAYS

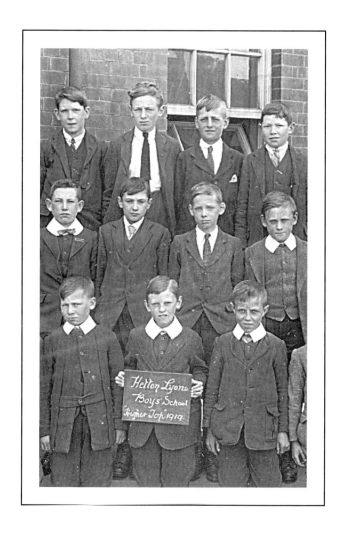

A class of Eppleton Colliery Infants School, *circa* 1905. The school stood on the site which is now grassed over and adjacent to the Downs Top Shop and Off Licence.

Eppleton Boys Football Team, 1918-19.

Hetton Lyons Primary School stands in a prominent position near Four Lane
Ends. This photograph was taken *circa* 1919. The building then contained
separate Boys', Girls' and Infants' Departments. In 1929 the school was
reorganised into Senior Mixed, Junior Mixed and Infant Schools. Later the
Senior Mixed became a Modern School, the Modern School moving to its own
site in 1967. In 1982 the Infant and Junior Schools merged to become the
Primary School. The School celebrated its 90th anniversary in 2002 with a
week of events which attracted over a thousand visitors.

One of the corridors at Hetton Lyons Boys' School, *circa* 1919.

Teaching Staff at Hetton Primary School, *circa* 1919. Seated centre is the Headmaster, Mr Heslop.

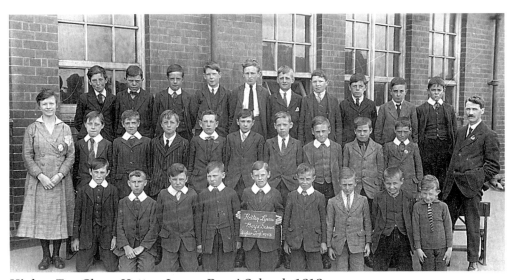

Higher Top Class, Hetton Lyons Boys' School, 1919.

Hetton Lyons Junior School Teaching Staff in 1973. Seated centre is the Heatdteacher, Mr Jack Steel, who later became Headteacher of the Primary School.

Hetton Lyons Primary School Band in 1985.

Hetton Lyons Primary School taking part in the National Spring Clean 2001.

A fire destroyed Eppleton Primary School in 1979. The school was subsequently re-built.

Hetton Library, formerly the Infants School. A plaque on the building reads: 'Originally built in 1873 as Hetton Infants School which was supported by the Hetton Coal Company. The school closed in the 1950s and was re-opened as the local branch library in 1961.'

The former Bog Row Girls' School, Hetton. It was opened in 1894. Much later it became a mixed school. It is now used by the City of Sunderland Social Services.

Hetton Secondary School, the area's Comprehensive School for eleven to sixteen-year-olds.

Hetton School – Visit to Derwent Hill in the Lake District, 1998.

SPORTS AND SPORTS PEOPLE

Bob Paisley outside Gateways in 1987. Born in Hetton he played in the Hetton Juniors' Football Team before the Second World War. He has been described as the most successful Manager in English Football. A plaque was placed on the Gateways building by Hetton Town Council which reads: 'To recognise the achievements in the Sport of Football with Liverpool FC of Bob Paisley, Manager Liverpool FC 1974-83.'

A boyhood photograph of Harry Potts of Houghton Road, Hetton, who became a professional footballer with Burnley. In a playing career that was interrupted by war the highlight was appearing in the 1947 FA Cup Final at Wembley. In 1950 he was transferred to Everton for £20,000. After spells as coach at Wolves and manager at Shrewsbury he returned to Burnley. He became one of the most successful managers in Burnley's history, leading them to the League championship in 1959-60 and FA Cup runners-up two years later. After a short stay at Blackpool he returned to Burnley for the 1977-79 seasons.

James Scott attended Eppleton Modern School where he displayed a remarkable talent for football. He played for England Schoolboys in 1949-50 (he is seen here in his England cap and playing strip). He later played League football for Burnley before moving on to Oldham Athletic. In the post-war period the North East was a rich source of talent for Burnley. James Scott was not the only Hetton lad to be snapped up by the Lancashire club, Ralph Coates went there in the 1960s and went on to play for England.

A Bowls Match in progress at Eppleton Colliery Welfare Park, *circa* 1931.

A Hetton Cricket Team, *circa* 1905.

Hetton Councillors' Cricket Match, July 1947.

A match on the Football Ground in Park View, 14th April 2002.

Sunday morning sports at Eppleton, September 2002.

Hetton Sports Centre. The foundation stone was laid by Councillor E. Kent, Chairman of Hetton Urban District Council on 21st April 1969, and the building officially opened on 15th April 1970 by Councillor J. Telford, the next Chairman of the Council.

A Gymkhana in the mid 1970s. The winding gear of Eppleton Colliery can be seen in the background.

Gymkhanas are still being held in the fields behind Hetton Community Centre. This photograph was taken in 2002 well after the closure of Eppleton Colliery so the landmark winding gear seen in the top photograph are no longer there. Not visible in this photograph are the vast windmills which now stand on the ridge and produce electric power.

A MUSICAL TRADITION

Left: Mr William Straughan of Church View Villas, Eppleton, with the author's father, Alan Berriman of Fence Houses, *circa* 1920. Mr Straughan was a teacher of musical instruments and conductor of Hetton Silver Prize Band and Sunderland Police Band. Alan Berriman became a very talented amateur classical violinist, winning numerous competitions.

Below: The Elmora Male Voice Choir, *circa* 1930. They were the forerunners of the celebrated Hetton Lyons Male Voice Choir.

Hetton Silver Prize Band 1947. The Band was formed in 1887. The present Band Hall in South Market Street was built in 1912. The first women members were admitted in the late 1950s and there is now a Junior (Learners) Group. Back row: E. Lawrence, J. Garside, R. Thompson, N. Lord, J. Bruce, R. Maddison, J. Bennett, W. Soulsby, E. Ellis. Middle row: J. Lawrence, A. Urwin, B. Speed, G. Davison, S. Thompson, E. Patterson, T. Coxon, J. Tatters, R. Dobson, T. Urwin. Front row: W. Urwin, C. Jackson, E. Sanderson, G. Scorer (Conductor for 30 years), R. Dawson, T.W. Urwin and H. Fletcher. The Urwin family was well represented in the Band. T.W. Urwin later became Member of Parliament for Houghton-le-Spring (1964-1983).

Hetton Silver Band 1994. 'Prize' has been dropped from the name, though it has been the winner of numerous competitions. Back row: J. Bell, S. Gibson, K. Smith, C. Bell, K. Trenbirth, C. Galley, K. Hagley, C. Heslop. Middle row: R. Gibson, G. Heslop, W. Smith, M. Meldrum, G. Wright, H. Huggard, G. Smith, D. Wilson, J. Buckingham (Secretary). Front row: T. Crisp, R. Gilchrist, M. Smith, N. Ibinson, K. Wheatley (Conductor), K. Price, M. Woodhouse, E. Buck (Treasurer) and P. Askew.

Hetton Silver Band at the Miners' Gala, Durham, 1986.

The Orchestra of Mr George Defty's Minstrel and Variety Show 1940/01 taken in the back yard of 9 Richard Street. Mr Defty is pictured far left.

Mr George Defty (centre) with members of his Concert Party.

A Concert Party run by Mrs Christina Carter, daughter of Mr George Defty.

Mr George Defty's Wartime Concert Party 1941. Mr Defty of 9 Richard Street, Hetton, was an accomplished pianist who for many years organised concert parties which raised funds in aid of voluntary organizations, and to help miners in peacetime and servicemen and women in wartime.

MEMORIES OF THE SECOND WORLD WAR

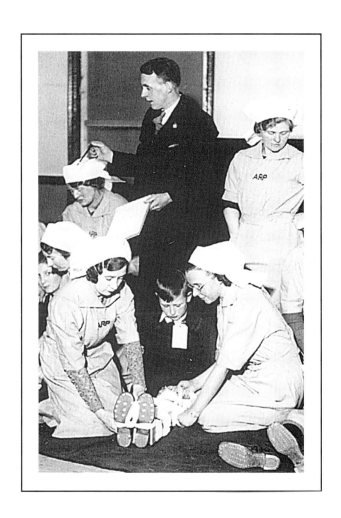

Collecting scrap metal in Hetton for the war effort, *circa* 1940. The Ministry of Aircraft Production asked for scrap metal to build aircraft, and vast amounts including pots and pans and wrought iron railings were collected throughout the country. During the Second World War, nearby Sunderland was heavily raided from the air by the Nazis between 1940 and 1943, and there were many air raid warnings in Hetton.

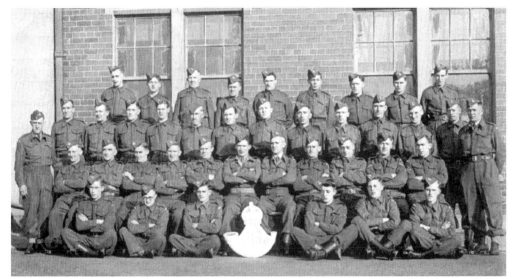

Hetton Home Guard, *circa* 1941. Originally called the Local Defence Volunteers the Home Guard recruited 500,000 men throughout the country between the ages of 17 and 65. Initially, their task was to assist in the defence of Great Britain against German Invasion. After the threat of invasion receded many were deployed in anti-aircraft work. The Home Guard was disbanded in 1944.

Hetton Auxiliary Fire Service, *circa* 1940. Note the sandbags.

A First Aid Demonstration in wartime Hetton, 1941.

Sisters Kathleen, Margaret and Christiana all served with the Women's Auxiliary Air Force, and were the daughters of Mr and Mrs George Defty of 9 Richard Street, Hetton.

Mr Harry Defty, son of Mr George Defty of Hetton, who served with the King's Own Scottish Borderers.

Mr George Defty Jnr at Nijmegen, Holland, December 1944.

Mr Peter Carter of Low Moorsley who served with the Royal Navy, and his wife Christiana (née Defty).

Mr George Kirkbride of Hetton who served in the Royal Army Service Corps.

At the end of the war in Europe streets all over the country held Victory Parties. Hetton was no exception. Richard Street Residents' Party was held in the Independent Methodist Chapel School Room in 1945.

The Avenue Victory Party, Hetton, 1945.

SECTION ELEVEN

RAIL, HORSE AND ROAD

The Lyons Cottages. A plaque fixed on the furthest cottage on the left says 'George Stephenson 1741-1848. Hetton Lyons Colliery opened in 1822. The colliery and railway were laid out by George Stephenson and built by his brother who lived in a cottage in this road. Plaque erected by Tyne & Wear County Council'. Referring to this railway in their book *Historical, Typographical, and Descriptive View of the County Palatine of Durham*, published in 1834, Mackenzie & Ross say: 'The operation of the powerful and ingenious machinery on this rail-way are truly wonderful. Five of Mr G. Stephenson's patent travelling engines, two 60 horse power, fixed reciprocating engines, and five self-acting inclined planes, simultaneously perform their various and complicated offices, with the precision and exactness of the most simple machinery. The whole arrangement of this new and wonderful undertaking was completed under the direction of Mr Robert Stephenson, the company's resident engineer.'

The Hetton Lyons Garage was originally built as an Engine Shed for Hetton Colliery Railway.

Right: A Pittington to Sunderland Train ready to depart from Hetton Station in 1950.

Left: A J39 Steam Engine with a Gala Day Special Train passes Hetton Signal Box and Goods Yard on 27th July 1951.

Hetton Station, *circa* 1915. In 1901 when Low Moorsley Amicable Industrial Society Limited ran an excursion train from Hetton to Redcar and Saltburn the adult return fare was two shillings and six pence. In 1949 the cheap day return fare from Hetton to Sunderland was three shillings and a penny first class, and one shilling and eleven pence third class. There was no such class as second. The station closed in 1953.

A Westwick's Milk Delivery Cart in Hetton, *circa* 1915.

A 20-Seater Hackney Carriage operated by S. Sparrow of Park Garage, Hetton, *circa* 1924.

The Petrol Station of Sydney Sparrow Ltd at Four Lane Ends, Hetton, in the 1950s. The Petrol Station is still there in 2002 and still owned by the same company.

Members of the Willis family of Hetton, well known for their long established Transport business, February 1960.

A van owned by John Speed, Tobacconists, outside the firm's premises in Richard Street, *circa* 1952.

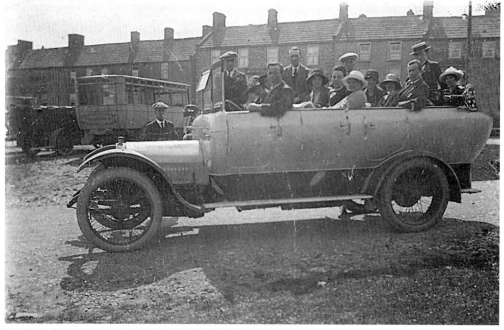

A Charabanc owned by E. & N. Ritchie at Hetton, *circa* 1914.

James Adam's Showroom at Station Road, Hetton, *circa* 1920. The Showroom was in the premises owned by E. & N. Richie, Haulage Contractors, who were established in 1889 and who occupy the building today. The founders, Mr Ernest and Mr Norman Ritchie, are in the photograph.

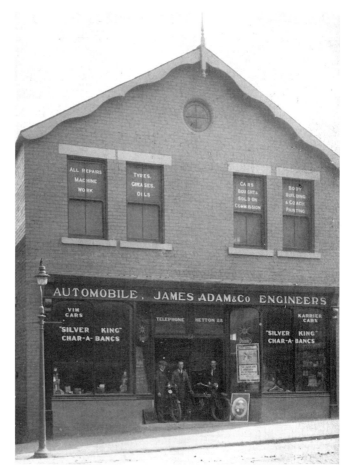

E. & N. Ritchie's premises at Station Road, *circa* 1960.

1936 Commer and 1939 Thornycroft Lorries owned by E. & N. Ritchie. Standing beside the Commer is Mr Ralph Blench, and the Thornycroft is Mr Matthew Hall.

Commer Tipper Lorry owned by E. & N. Ritchie and used by the Hetton Sand & Gravel Company. Beside the Commer is Mr Victor Last.

Bibliography

Churches of the Diocese of Durham Edited by Canon John Roscoe

Coal Mining in County Durham by Durham County Environmental Education Curriculum Group in co-operation with *The Northern Echo*

Banners of the Durham Coalfield by Norman Emery published by Sutton Publishing 1998

The Durham Miners 1919-60 by W.R. Aside published by George Allen & Unwin

Kelly's Directory of County Durham 1925

Historical, Typographical & Descriptive View of the County Palatine of Durham by Mackenzie & Ross published by Mackenzie & Dent 1834

Lost Houses of County Durham by Peter Meadows and Edward Waterson published by Jill Raines 1993

The Macmillan Dictionary of the Second World War by Elizabeth-Anne Whitehead and Stephen Pope (Consultant Editor Professor Keith Robbins) 2nd Edition 1997

The Place Names of Northumberland and Durham by Allan Mawer published by Cambridge University Press 1920

The Place Names of County Durham by Ian Stuart Robson published by Leighton House 1998

The Concise Oxford Dictionary of English Place Names 4th Edition 1959 by Eilert Ekwall published by Oxford at the Clarendon Press

Hetton-le-Hole Independent Methodist Church – An Illustrated Church History by Shaun Newton 2001

The Forgotten Railway – An Article by J.T. Kavanagh, Hetton-le-Hole

The Buildings of England County Durham by Nikolaus Pevsner published by Penguin Books First Edition 1953

Houghton-le-Spring and Hetton-le-Hole in Old Photographs, First (1989) and Second (1991) Selections by Ken Richardson published by Alan Sutton Publishing Limited

Pocket Atlas, Topography and Gazetteer of England Pigot & Co 1821

The History and Antiquities of the County Palatine of Durham Vol 1 by R. Surtees 1816

Ribbons and Medals by Captain H. Taprell Dorling published by George Philip & Son Second Impression 1963

Hetton Lyons Primary School 1912-2002 90th Birthday by Alan Thomas 2002

Form 6, Hetton Lyons Girls' School, 1919.

The People's History

To receive a catalogue of our latest titles send a large SAE to:

The People's History
Suite 1
Byron House
Seaham Grange Business Park
Seaham
County Durham
SR7 0PY

www.thepeopleshistory.co.uk